The Oxford Piano Method

P·I·A·N·O T·I·M·E J·A·Z·Z

Book 2

Pauline Hall

MUSIC DEPARTMENT

OXFORD
UNIVERSITY PRESS

OXFORD
UNIVERSITY PRESS

Great Clarendon Street, Oxford OX2 6DP, England
198 Madison Avenue, New York, NY10016, USA

Oxford University Press is a department of the University of Oxford.
It furthers the University's aim of excellence in research, scholarship,
and education by publishing worldwide

Oxford is a registered trade mark of Oxford University Press
in the UK and in certain other countries

24

ISBN 0–19–372734–X 978–0–19–372734–2

Illustrations by Andy Hammond

Music and text origination by
Barnes Music Engraving Ltd., East Sussex
Printed in Great Britain on acid-free paper by
Halstan & Co. Ltd., Amersham, Bucks.

Contents

Reggae stamp

FIONA MACARDLE

With a strong beat

Warm starry nights

STEPHEN DURO

Slow beguine

Clear water

DAVID BLACKWELL

Late at night

FIONA MACARDLE

Sleepy

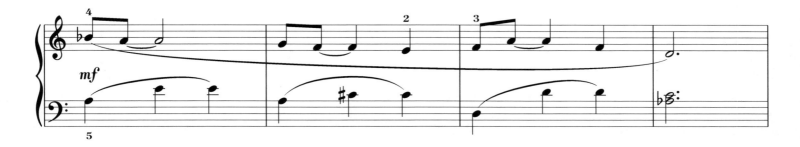

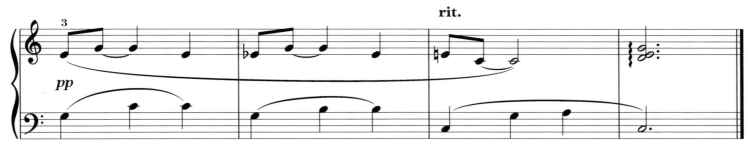

Ped.

High Street blues

ALAN BULLARD

Rhythmic and heavy

Waltz for Alice

ROY STRATFORD

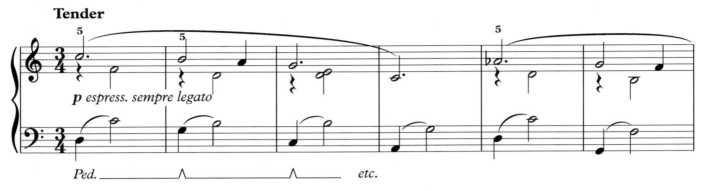

Snowball rag

FIONA MACARDLE

Star gazing

ALAN BULLARD

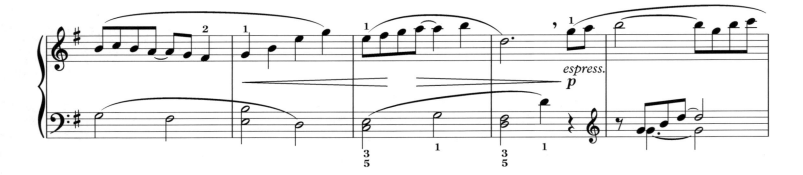

Chase in the dark

DAVID BLACKWELL

Three-quarter time

ALAN BULLARD

Funfair

PAULINE HALL

With a swing (♩♪ = ♪³♪)

Ol' man boogie blues

PETER GRITTON

Ponderous, but rhythmic

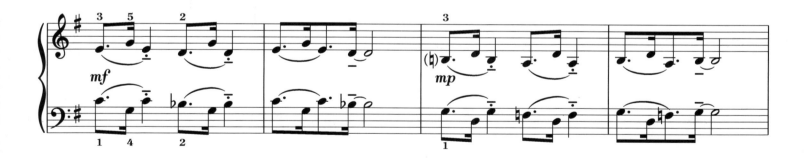

Head in the clouds

ALAN BULLARD

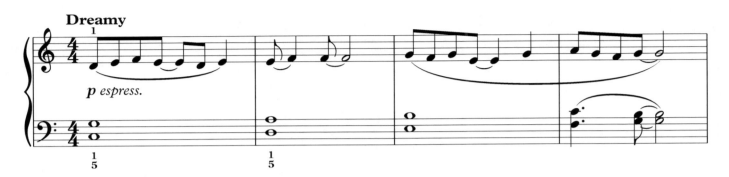

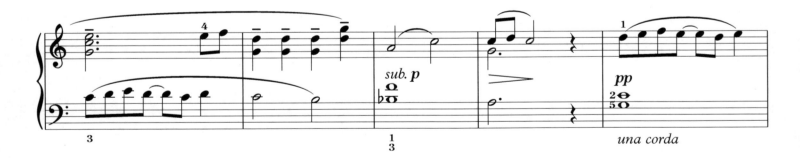

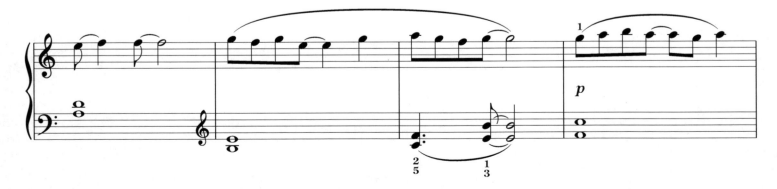

Moody Max

DAVID BLACKWELL

Go with the flow

ALAN BULLARD

Tango Argentina

PAULINE HALL

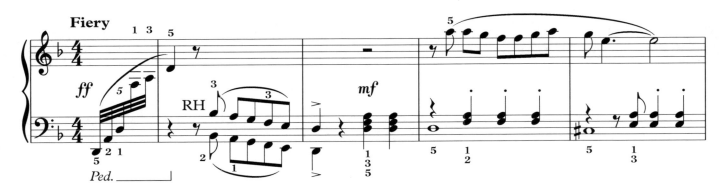

Railroad blues

DAVID BLACKWELL

23

Whistle stop

PAUL DRAYTON

RH 8ve higher throughout

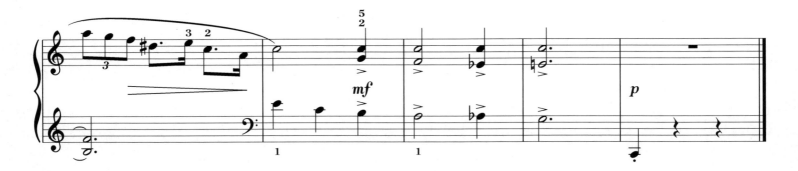

Cat's eyes

DAVID BLACKWELL

With menace

Polka dots

DAVID BLACKWELL

Round the bend

ALAN BULLARD

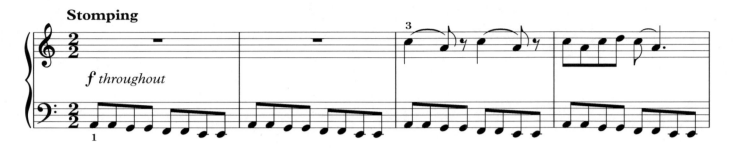

Promise!

RODERICK SKEAPING

'Give us a bite!' 'Ask me nice-ly!' 'Give us a bite!' 'Ask me nice-ly!'

'Give us a bite!' 'Ask me nice-ly!' 'Come on, Mum!' I'm hun-gry!

Give us a bite!' 'Ask me nice-ly!' 'Give us a bite!' 'Ask me nice-ly!' 'Give us a bite!'

'Ask me nice-ly!' 'Come on, Mum! Please feed me!' 'Pro-mise you won't leave it?

Pro-mise you won't spill it? Pro-mise you won't heave it on the cat or

This isn't as hard as it looks! Use the words to help you with the rhythm and say them in time before you start to play.

dog?'   'Pro-mise I won't   leave it!   Pro-mise I won't   spill   it!

Pro-mise I won't   heave it   on   the cat   or   dog!'   'O.   K!'

Warm up

ROY STRATFORD

Bright

Lively lion

KEVIN WOODING

Rock steady